1986

To: J.J.

christmas of almost 4 years

Love

Mom & Dad

Translated by Donald Maclean

First published in German under the title *Federleicht* by Verlag Urachhaus, Stuttgart, 1985.
First published in English in 1986 by Floris Books.

© Verlag Urachhaus Johannes Mayer GmbH & Co KG Stuttgart
This translation © Floris Books, Edinburgh, 1986.
All rights reserved. No part of this publication may be reproduced
without the prior permission of Floris Books, 21 Napier Road, Edinburgh.

British Library Cataloguing in Publication data available

ISBN 0–86315–033–0

Printed in West Germany

Featherlight

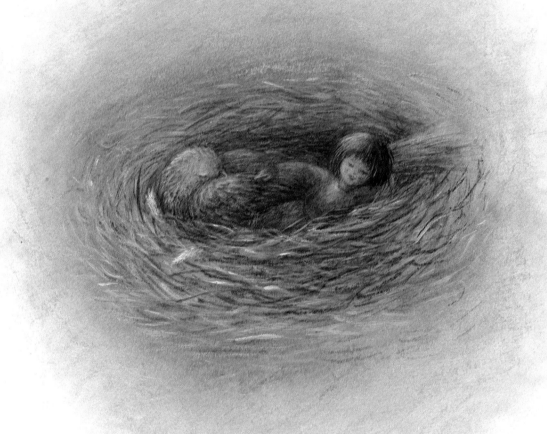

Story and pictures
by
Gabriele Gernhard Eichenauer

Floris Books

There was once a little boy who was very small and delicate. He just did not grow one little bit. It worried his mother and father, so they took him into the country where the sky was blue and the sun was always smiling. There Grandmother had a garden where the little boy felt happy and safe. She called him "Featherlight" because he was so small and light.

All the birds from far and near came to the garden, for in it there were many sunflowers that grew thick and tall like a wood. Featherlight liked to gather the sunflower seeds to feed his feathered friends when winter came. Best of all he loved the smallest bird with the golden feathers, for it was quite tame and sang the loveliest songs.

Sometimes Grandmother sat on the garden bench in the sun. She told stories about the time, long ago, when she was a child, or of how she used to go to market with Grandfather to sell flowers and seeds. Featherlight loved to listen. He used to sit on one knee while Golden Bird perched on the other. They would share the sunflower seeds in the basket that lay on Grandmother's lap.

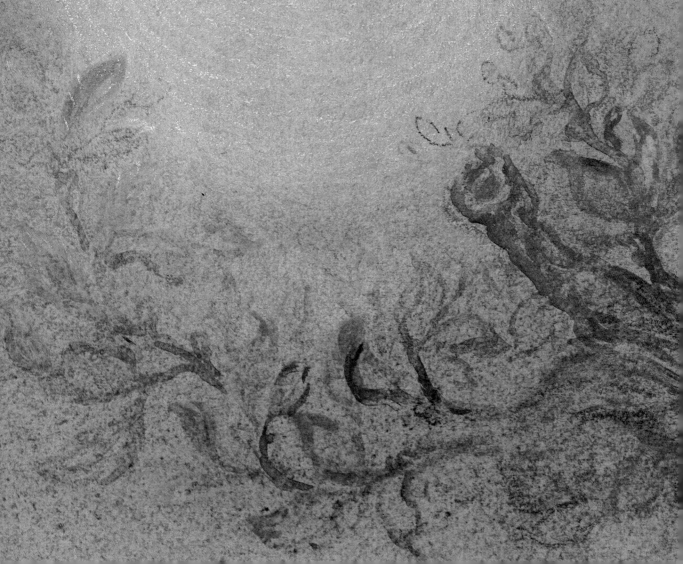

In the evening, when the sun had set and the moon was high in the sky, Featherlight and Golden Bird snuggled down in Golden Bird's warm and cozy nest. During the night Featherlight would dream that Golden Bird was really a child too, and together they ran through the garden, playing hide-and-seek in the forest of sunflowers.

Featherlight was happy and contented. Only in the morning, when Golden Bird flew high up into the sky and disappeared in the distance, Featherlight grew sad and sighed, "Oh, why does Golden Bird always fly away into the wide, wide world?" How he longed for her to come back.

As soon as Golden Bird came home she would tell him about her adventures. Gaily she described the farmer in the field, the fisherman on the river, brightly-coloured berries in the wood, and how she had just managed to escape from a dangerous cat.

"Come with me tomorrow," sang Golden Bird. "You're as light as a feather, I'll take you on my back and show you the world."

But Featherlight was afraid and said he would rather stay at home.

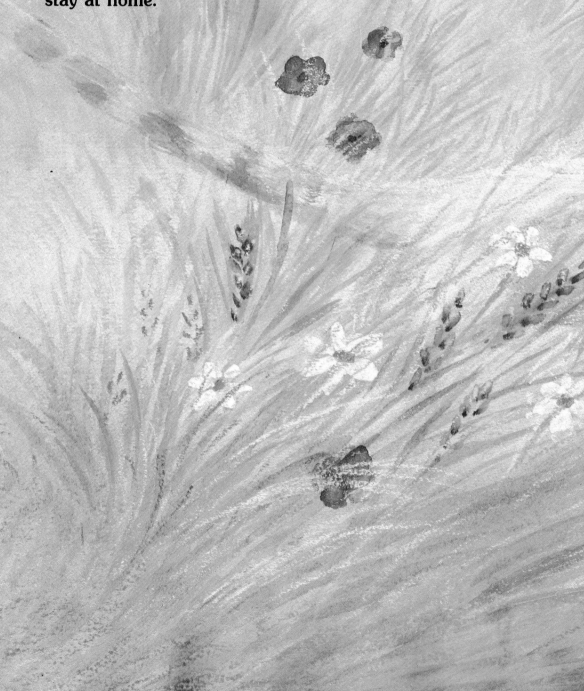

But one day Golden Bird did not come back. Featherlight waited and waited. By now the sun was low in the sky and he was very anxious. At last he climbed the tallest sunflower to look for her. He could see far beyond Grandmother's garden, but Golden Bird was nowhere to be found. Just as he was beginning to give up hope and run to Grandmother, he saw a dove far away in the distance.

Nearer and nearer the dove came until at last it alighted beside him.

"Croo, croo," cooed the dove. "I have come from the town. Golden Bird has sent me. She is in great trouble and needs your help. Only you can save her."

Featherlight looked distressed. "Where is Golden Bird?" he cried. "How can I help her? Take me to her quickly!"

He ran to get the seed basket in case Golden Bird was hungry and then climbed on the dove's back. He could not stop thinking of Golden Bird and of what might have happened.

Very soon they could see the spires of the town. The dove flew to a windowsill. Featherlight slid from its back, crept through the open window and hid behind the curtain. Cautiously he peeped out and his heart nearly stood still. There was Golden Bird shut up in a cage!

A gloomy grey man was holding the cage tight saying: "No, I won't let you out again. Now at last I am no longer alone. You'll have to sing for me. Why don't you sing, you stupid bird?"

The old man put the cage down and left the room with downcast eyes and drooping shoulders.

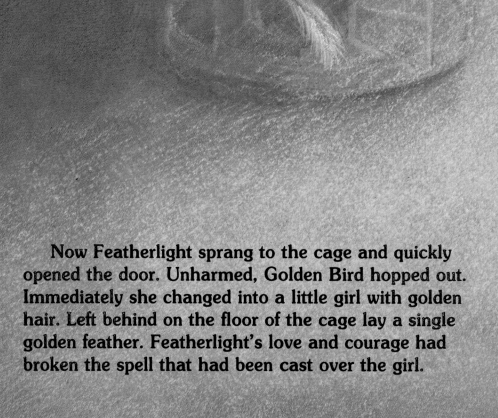

Now Featherlight sprang to the cage and quickly opened the door. Unharmed, Golden Bird hopped out. Immediately she changed into a little girl with golden hair. Left behind on the floor of the cage lay a single golden feather. Featherlight's love and courage had broken the spell that had been cast over the girl.

Outside the dove was waiting. Swiftly she carried the children back to Grandmother's garden. But in all their joy and excitement they had quite forgotten about the basket with the seeds. It was left standing by the window.

From that day on the two children gathered seeds and cared for the garden together. The sunflowers nodded gently as they reached up towards the sun. And Featherlight and Golden Bird grew bigger and stronger every day. Soon they were able to take flowers and seeds to market all by themselves and they helped to look after Grandmother too. She was growing old and could no longer walk all the way into the town.

Every morning an old man came to the market to buy a basket full of sunflower seeds from the children. He was not gloomy and grey anymore but gave them a friendly smile. In his buttonhole he wore a golden feather. Often he would tell them of his friends, the birds, who sang the loveliest songs because every day he scattered seeds for them on his windowsill.